Rock of Snow

By RL Lane

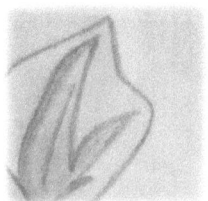

ISBN: 1517679478
ISBN-13: 978-1517679477

Illustrations and Photo Cover by RL Lane

"Every time I get sick I think I am not going to get better and I am going to die. I hate being sick. I don't want to do anything. It reminds me of the last few years of my Mom's life. She was sick every day. I only remember one day in all those days when she said she felt good. Just one day. I don't know how she did it. My Dad's boxing name was "The Rock", but she was the real rock." RL Lane

Human perseverance is like nothing else. Just keep going on…

The human mind is like nothing else. Just keep thinking on…

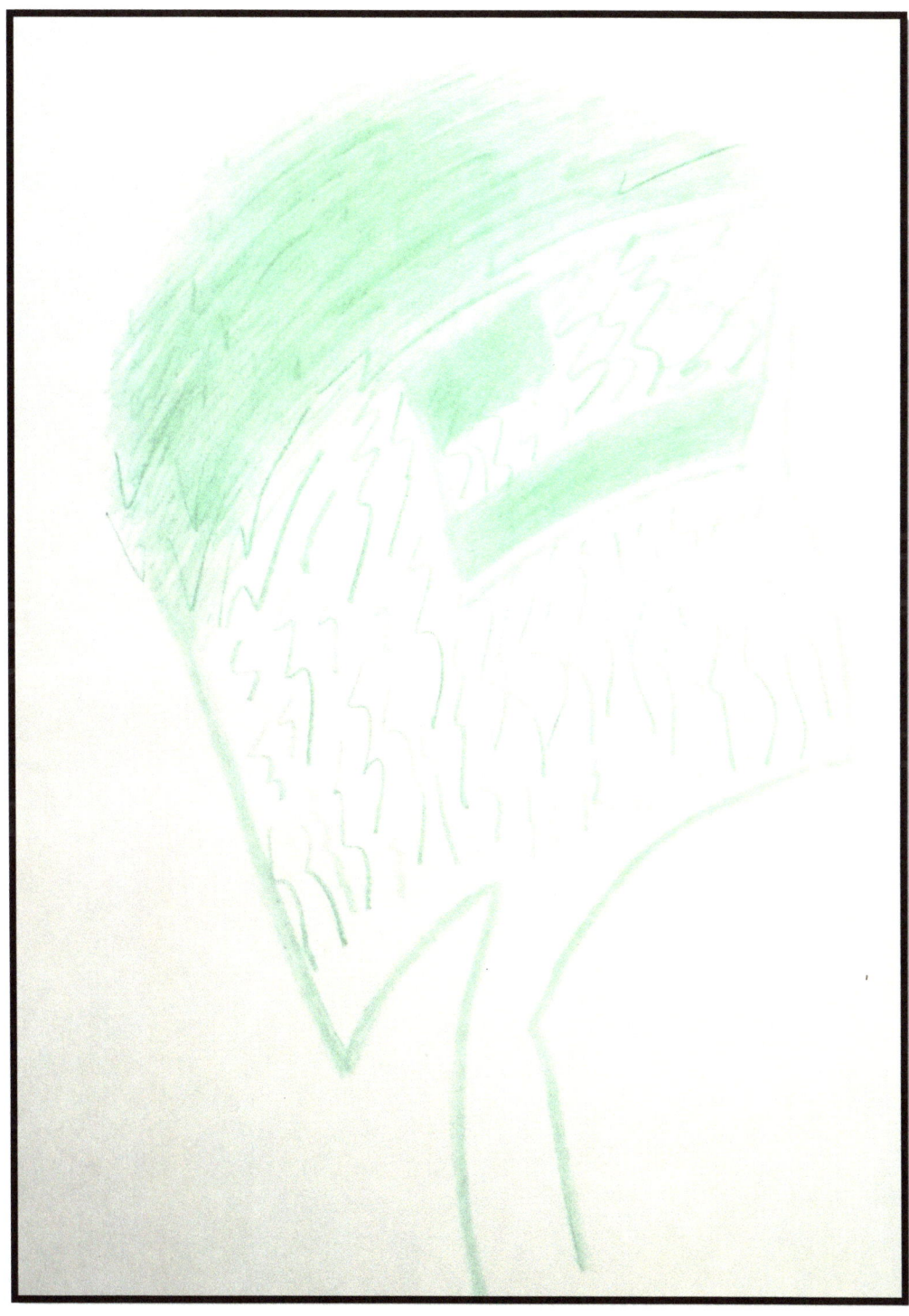

I have only one picture of my Dad wearing his boxing gloves. It is on old newspaper clipping. I like to look at the younger man who had a lot of fight in him…

Jab to the right

Jab to the left

He showed you how

Why did you forget?

That was part of one of the poems in EcarreT where I wrote about all the events that occurred to change my life. For the better…

The stars aligned and changed my life beyond any of my wildest dreams…

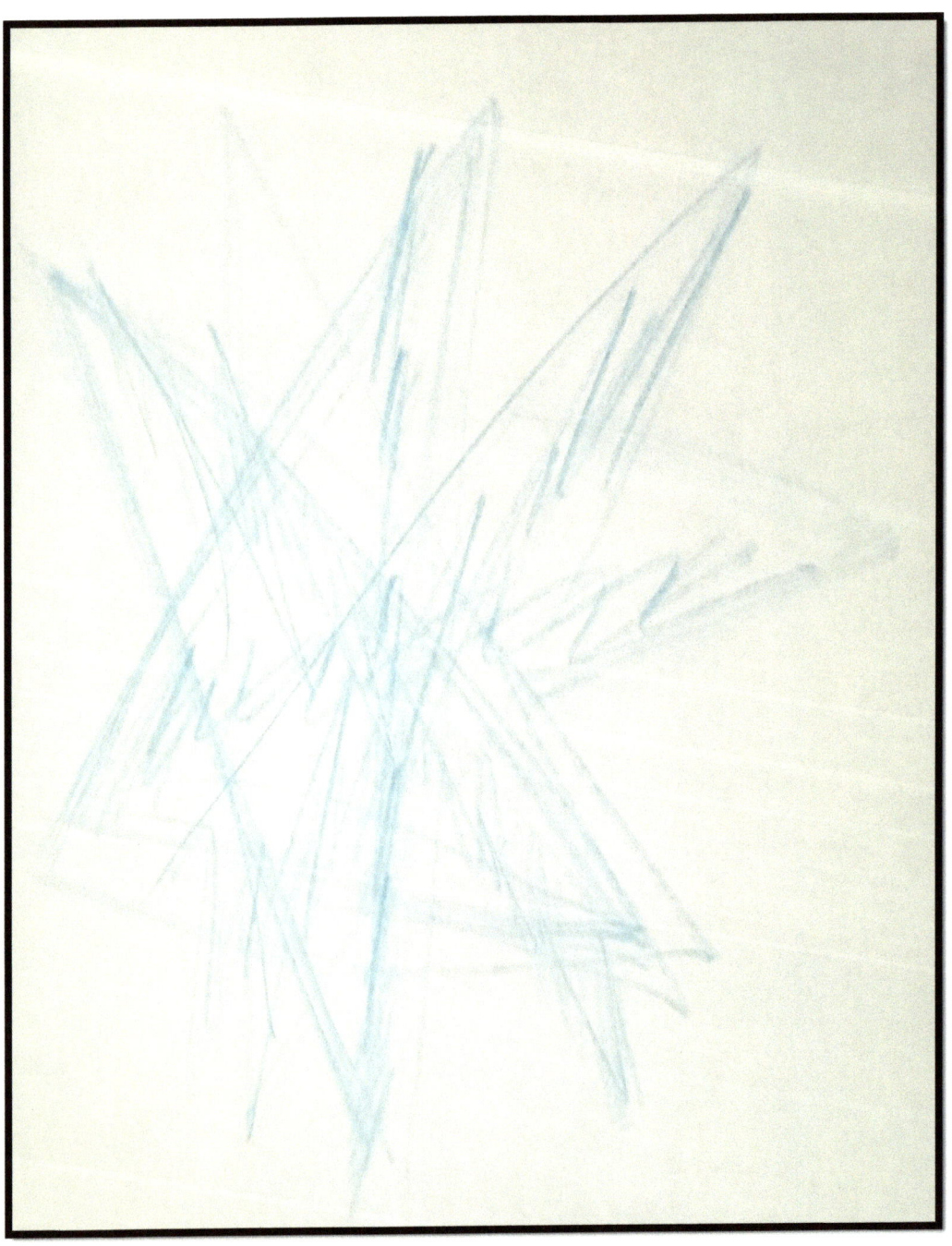

I love to think of parents reading "G" or "How to Catch A Goast" to their children. I like to think of them talking about the story…looking at the pictures or wondering about the words…

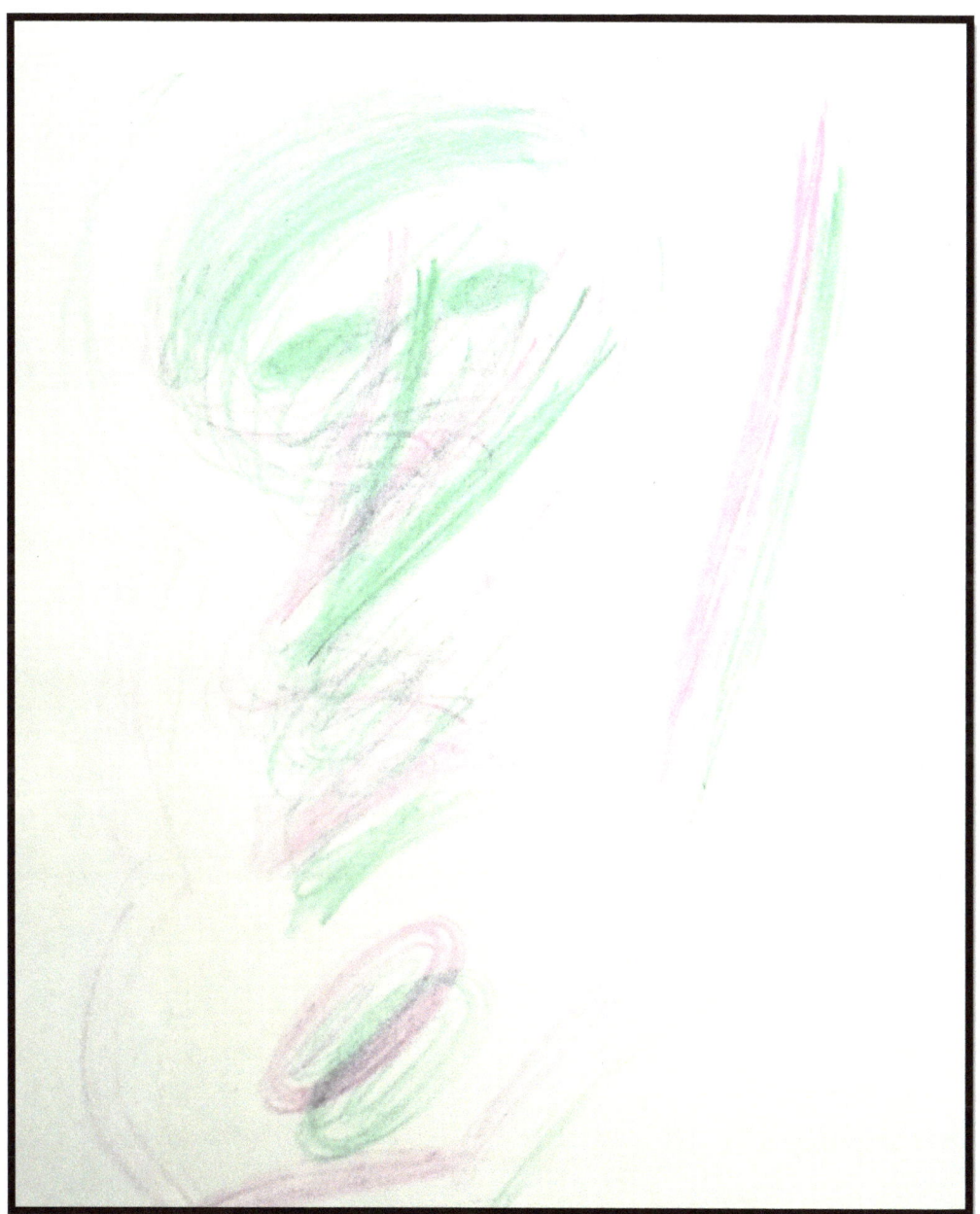

I draw the pictures simply by hand on a piece of paper. With a pen or pencil or crayon or colored pencil or marker and then take a picture of them to load into the book document…

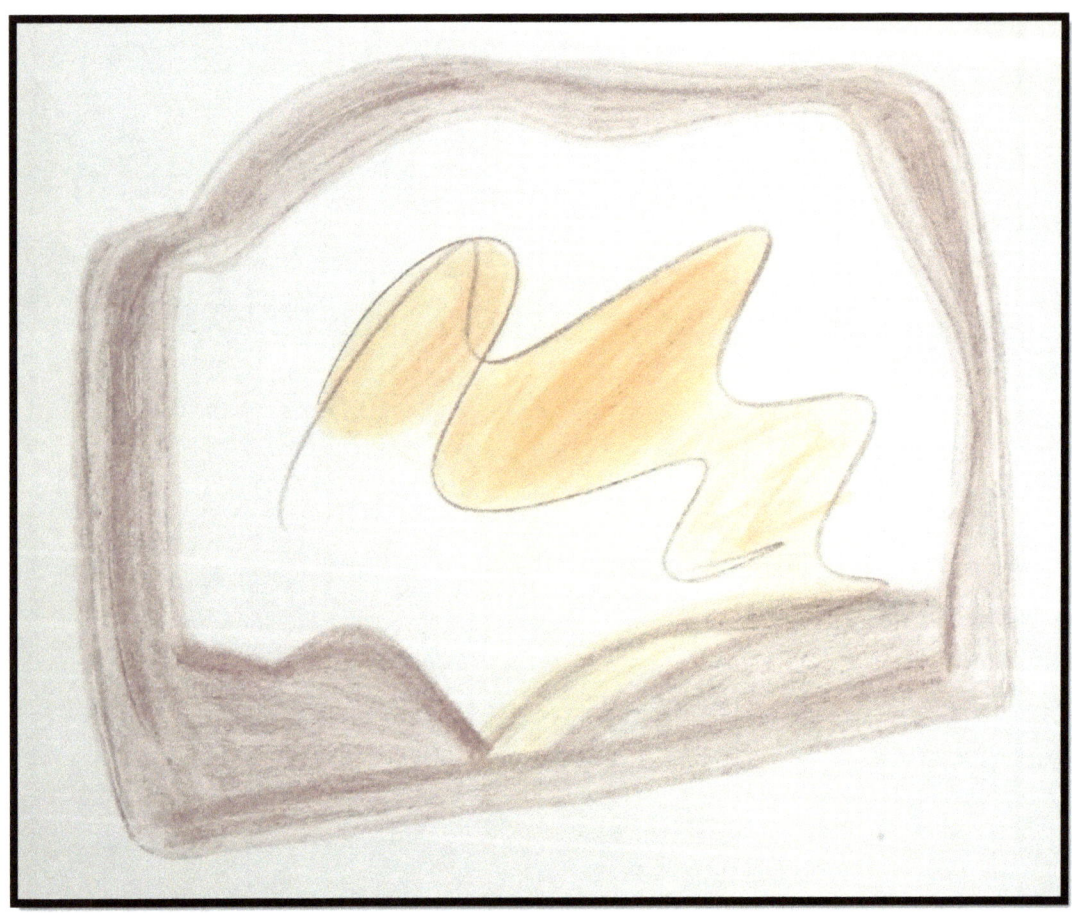

The drawing on the front cover is a snowman made of rocks. He would be the strongest most durable snowman ever. He would not melt…

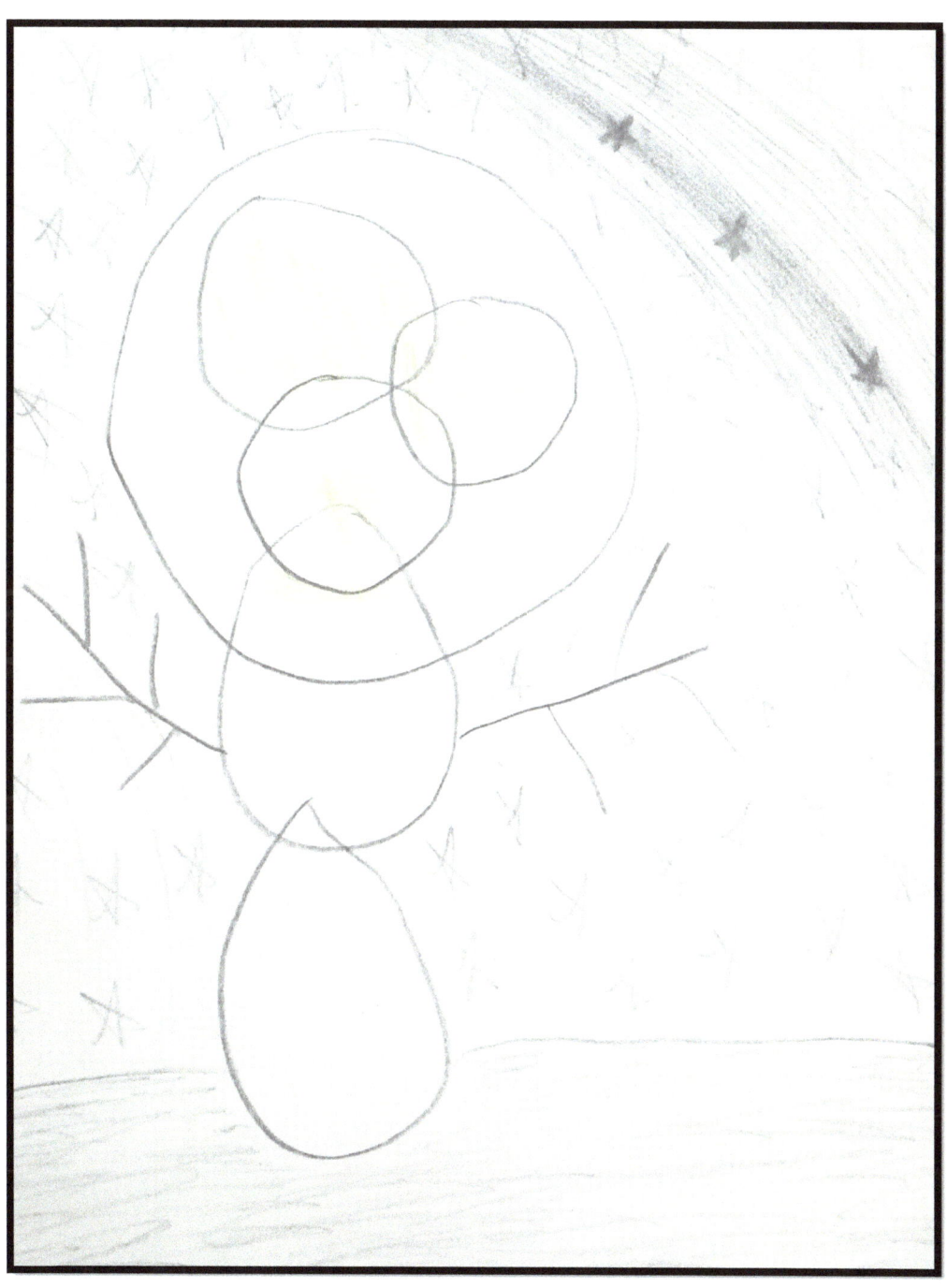

In the EcarreT series, the "rock" is our earth. The series tracks the lives of many people and the difference they made during their short time on this rock. It is about perseverance. It is about love. It is about hope. It is also sad. It tells the sad stories so people can be helped…

The snow is going to soon be falling again. Many states will be a rock of snow. The cold will be back. I hate the cold. If I were to draw the cold, it would be an ugly thing with harsh edges and unpleasant colors…

I don't like to think of all the homeless in the cold. I see them every day as I walk to work. Hard cold cement. Frozen noses and frostbit fingers. Why can't we all have a home?

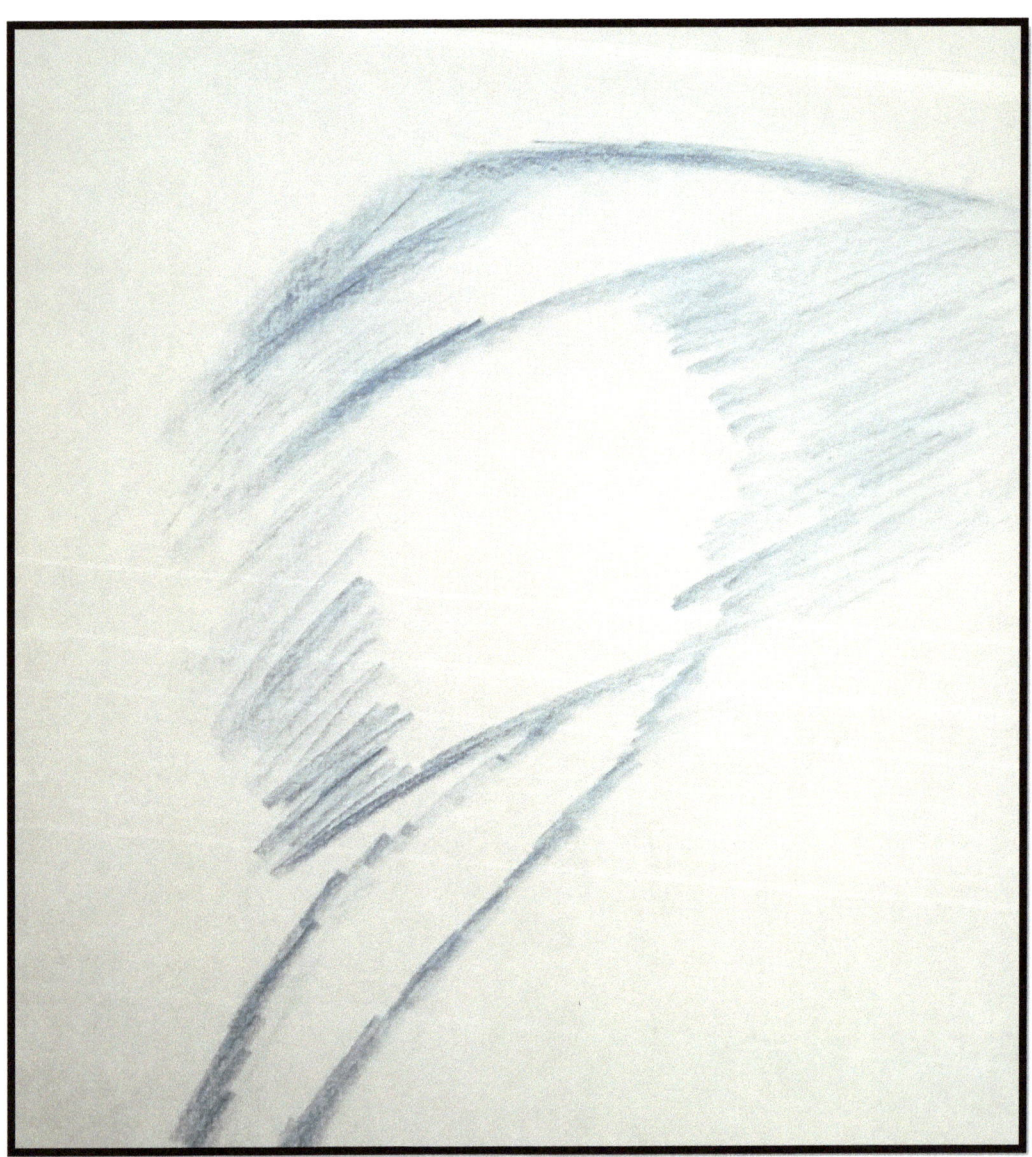

The animals too. Why can't they all have houses? I don't think their brains can comprehend why they have to live without a home…

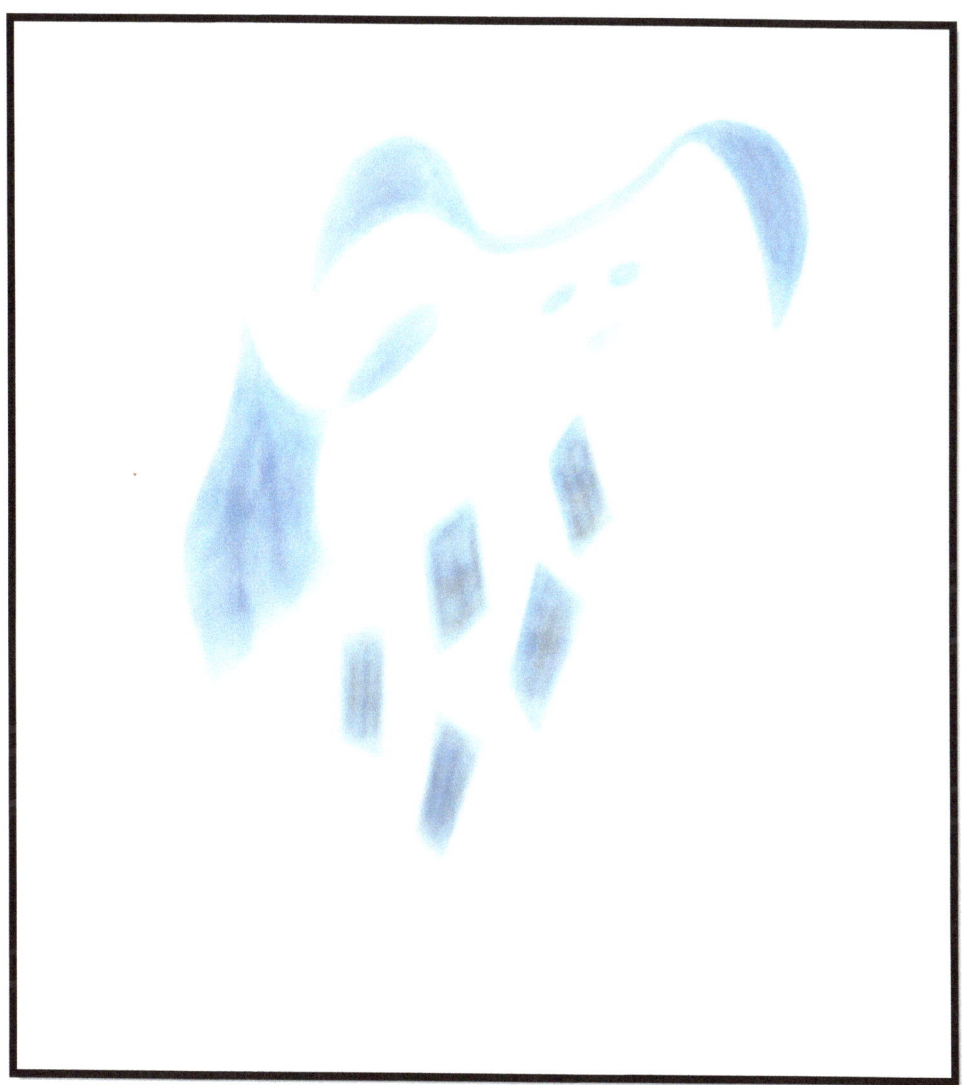

So is this all about homes? The homes on the rock…on the earth. The homes we come back to at the end of the day. The homes we never leave because our job is there too. The homes where we hide and where we learn to come out. The homes where we cry and help each other out. The homes where we eat and where we go to sleep. Where we refresh…before we go back out…to the rock…

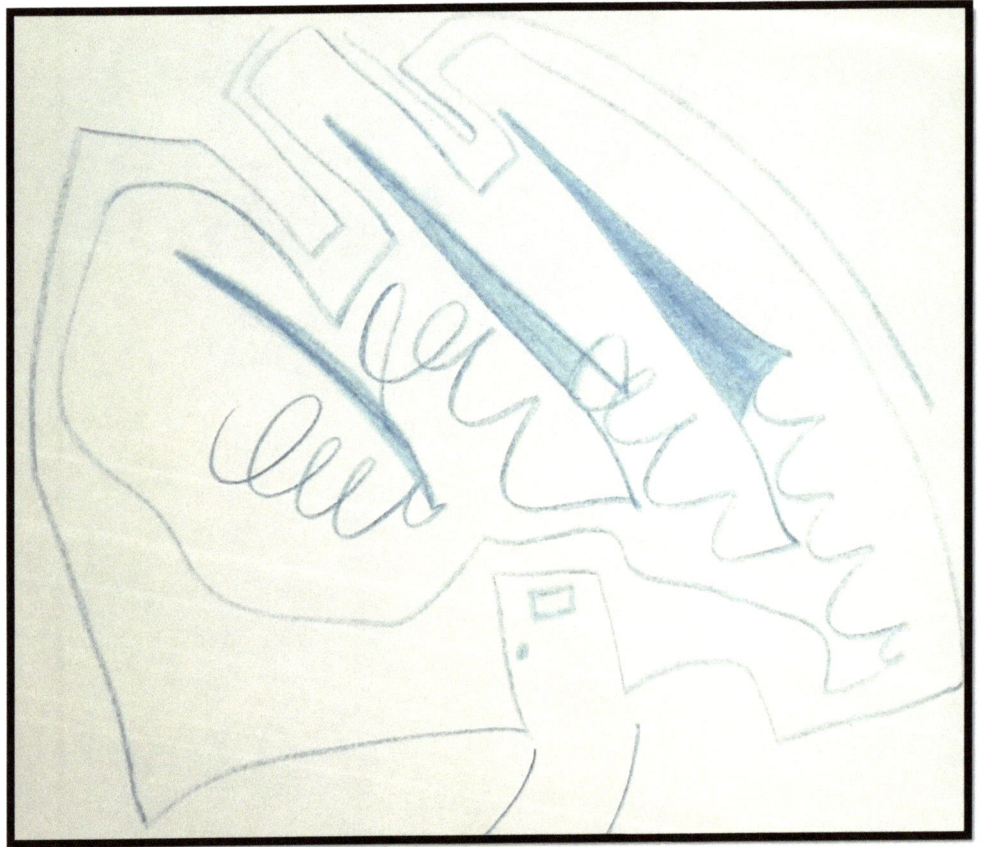

No.

The real message of this story…value your health. Do want…what you can to keep it at its best for as long as you can. You will want a lot less things when you have lost your health…

Dedicated to the real rock.

Will the real rock please stand up?

Take a bow

You deserve a hand

You fought against all odds

Persevered till the end

Even when doom and gloom prevailed

Many around you had already given up

But somehow you didn't

It's funny your name was the same as what drove you...

faith.

About the Author and Illustrator

RL Lane has published the EcarreT series and a collection of short stories featuring the illustrations, along with the children's books "G" and "How to Catch a Goast". The series begins with "Chapel Street Signs"...

...unexplained connections that challenge us to beli ve. A woman, a Dad a Doctor, a cat and mouse, a horse and tale tell their stories. "Do you beli ve in spirits?" I asked my friend. "Well look", he said, "I believe there are things that cannot be explained..." Oh. Plus, hear ov a Mom's battle with her struggle to connect to the woman...her little girl.

Welcome to EcarreT...a world
Where everyone cares
Why did I have to create it in...

A fiction fantasy world?

You may already know why, but you will see regardless of what you believe as a girl's journey of love and faith on her "Touring Machine" take her on the best journey of her mundane life. A life well on its way takes a turn in a direction that could've never been seen or even dreamed...

The author can be contacted at:

RosaLeeeLane@gmail.com
www.Amazon.com/author/readrllane

Twitter.com/readrllane

Books by RL Lane

Chapel Street Signs

secret Life OV an antE

Sri Town

Which of EcarreT

Hand of Heven

Short Stories:

Mon Treal, The Odd Cod, The Half Day, No Gift for Greed, Aunt Elm & Uncle Poc, What Would Caitlin Wear, The Bag of Scribbles, Mr. Uraly's Italy, A not G, Johnni and Georg, A Cup of Butter, The Walk of a THOUSAND Moods, Storm Window, The Rugs, Cones of Ice Crème, Angel-A, The Art of Sri Town, Under Water, The Dinner Party, The Vault, No Lines to Erase

Children's:

G

How to Catch a Goast

www.ingramcontent.com/pod-product-compliance
Lightning Source LLC
Chambersburg PA
CBHW050433180526

45159CB00006B/2515